FEMINISM

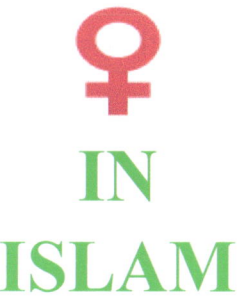

IN
ISLAM

Akhtar A. Alvi, PE

**Razia Akhtar Alvi Institute
For Empowering Studies
Lahore, Pakistan**

CONTENTS

DEDICATION 5

ACKNOWLEDGMENTS 6

CHAPTER 1 WHY WRITE THIS BOOK? 7

CHAPTER 2 FEMINISM 8

CHAPTER 3 FEMINISM WAVES 11

CHAPTER 4 FEMINISM HISTORY 14

CHAPTER 5 PATRIARCHY 17

CHAPTER 6 RELIGION AND FEMINISM 19

CHAPTER 7 ISLAMIC FEMINISM 22

CHAPTER 8 ISLAMIC JUSTICE 24

CHAPTER 9 ISLAMIC RIGHTS MARRIAGE AND DIVORCE .. 29

CHAPTER 10 ABORTION IN ISLAM 38

CHAPTER 11 ISLAMIC PROPERTY DISTRIBUTION ... 41

CHAPTER 12 ISLAMIC DEBT 44

CHAPTER 13 WOMEN IN ISLAM 47

CHAPTER 14 SEX IN ISLAM 57

CHAPTER 15 USA FEMINISM GOAL 64

CHAPTER 16 FEMISISM OF DR. IQBAL 67

CHAPTER 17 PROGRESS 72

CHAPTER 18 CONCLUSION 73

BIBLIOGRAPHY 80

APPENDIX 81

AUTHOR 96

COPYRIGHT © 2024

Feminism In Islam
By
Akhtar A. Alvi, P.E.

eBook ISBN: 978-1-966003-35-9
Paperback ISBN: 979-8-326402-36-3
Hardback ISBN: 979-8-326402-46-2

All rights are reserved. No part of this book may be used or reproduced by any means, graphic, electronic, or mechanical, including photocopying, recording, taping, or by any information storage retrieval system without the written permission of the author except in the case of brief quotations embodied in critical articles and reviews.

This book is sold subject to the conditions that it shall not, by way of trade or otherwise, be lent, re-sold, hired out, or otherwise circulated without the author's prior consent in any form of binding or cover other than that in which it is published.

ALVI FAMILY PORTRAIT - 1983

- Back: Left to right - Razia, Akhtar
- Front: Anwar, Rizwan (elder son)
- Immigrated to the USA in 1976. Anwar was 6 weeks old, and Rizwan was 20 ½ months old.

DEDICATION

To the late Razia Akhtar Alvi, who was my life partner and love of my life for 50 years. She passed away on Wednesday, March 13, 2019. God, please,

- Bless her soul and family.
- Allow us to live together again in paradise in our eternal life.

ACKNOWLEDGMENTS

I am grateful to:

- Google and Wikipedia for the use of their free internet material.
- My:
  - Scholar-friend Mubasher Ahmad for editing the book.
  - Friend Naveed Malik for the jacket design.
  - My friends Epcon CEO Aziz Jamaluddin and business partner Dr. Ali Kamran Rana and his team for their review with valuable suggestions.
- The team at Turner Book Writers for publishing, marketing, and selling the book.

CHAPTER 1

WHY WRITE THIS BOOK?

My mother gave me birth, breastfed me for months, and lay awake at night when I was sick. She trained me to go to the bathroom and walked with me to my first school. She shaped me into the person I am today.

I had two grandmothers, two sisters, and multiple aunts. At work, I had women colleagues. In my 83-year life, I have had many female friends.

It hurts to know that historically, women have been considered second-class citizens. They had to, and still do, fight for their rights.

I thought they had and should have more rights than men. Without women giving birth to children, there will be no mankind and humanity. If the women were to decide to have no more pregnancies, in a few decades, the human race would cease to exist

I consider God's creation of women to be the foundation of His creation. They are like the roots of a tree. Without a root, there would be no tree, its stem, and leaves to have a shade to shelter humans from the scorching heat of the sun.

In writing this book, my objective is to look at the history of feminism, its current status, and its place in Islam.

CHAPTER 2

FEMINISM

Feminism is:

- The advocacy of women's rights and the pursuit of gender equality.
- Movements initiated by/for women define and establish the political, economic, personal, and social equality of the sexes.
- About:
    - Promoting equal rights and opportunities for all genders
    - Respecting the diverse experiences, identities, knowledge, and strengths of women and striving to empower them eventually leads to the realization of their full rights.

Feminism Goal and Campaign
The goal of feminism is to challenge the systemic inequalities women face on a daily basis. It campaigns for women's rights to:

- Vote.
- Run for the public office.
- Work.
- Earn equal pay.
- Own property.
- Receive education.
- Enter contracts.
- End oppression.
- Achieve gender equality in law and in practice.

- Protection against sexual harassment and assault.
- Have:
    - Reproductive rights.
    - Equal rights within marriage.
    - Maternity leave.

Feminism Theory
Feminism theory analyzes gender inequality, discrimination, objectification (including sexual objects), oppression, patriarchal (men domination), stereotyping (a wrong set idea), and performativity (out of convention).

Types Of Feminism
There are six types of feminism:

1. Mainstream
2. Liberal
3. Radical
4. Cultural
5. Marxist and Socialist
6. Difference

Mainstream feminism focuses on institutional reforms for reducing gender discrimination, giving women access to male-dominated spaces, and promoting equality.

Liberal feminism, or the equality approach, has been the leading form of feminism in the U.S. and much of Western Europe since English feminist Mary Wollstonecraft's vigorous call for equality for women in her 1792 book *Vindication of the Rights of Woman*.

Radical feminists view society as fundamentally patriarchal in which men dominate and oppress women.

Cultural feminism claims the existence of a "female nature" or "female essence" and seeks to reevaluate and redefine attributes ascribed to femaleness.

Marxist feminism is an anti-colonial and anti-imperialist movement. It mobilizes feudal relations of gender oppression to capture populations, land, and markets. Socialist feminism has been developed from these precepts in a range of ways around the world.

Difference feminism asserts that there are differences between women and men, but no value judgment can be placed upon them, and both sexes possess equal moral status as individuals.

CHAPTER 3

FEMINISM WAVES

There have been four feminism waves:

1. 1848 - 1920.
2. 1963 - 1980s.
3. 1990s – 2010s.
4. Present Day.

The first wave of feminism focused on property rights and the right to vote. In the US, first-wave feminism is considered to have ended with the passage of the 19th Amendment to the United States Constitution in 1919, granting women the right to vote in all states.

The second wave of feminism centered on equality and anti-discrimination. In 1963, Betty Friedan's book "*The Feminine Mystique*" helped articulate the discontent felt by American women. The book is credited with sparking the beginning of second-wave feminism in the United States. Within 10 years, women comprised over half of the global workforce.

The third wave feminism:

- Started in the 1990s as a response to the perceived privileging of white, straight women in the second wave.
- Embraces the belief in two separate and opposing genders with associated natural roles that match their assigned sex while acknowledging that heterosexuality is often taken for granted. This perspective is pervasive and persistent, carrying negative consequences.
- Gained momentum through Anita Hill's televised testimony in 1991 before an all-white male Senate Judiciary Committee. She accused Clarence Thomas, nominated for the Supreme Court of the United States, of

sexual harassment. Credit for the emergence of third-wave feminism goes to Rebecca Walker, who responded to Thomas's appointment to the Supreme Court with an article in Ms. Magazine titled "*Becoming the Third Wave*" (1992). She wrote:

> "I write this as a plea to all women, especially women of my generation: Let Thomas' confirmation serve to remind you, as it did to me, that the fight is far from over. Let this dismissal of a woman's experience move you to anger. Turn that outrage into political power. Do not vote for them unless they work for us. Do not have sex with them, do not break bread with them, and do not nurture them if they don't prioritize our freedom to control our bodies and our lives. I am not a post-feminism feminist. I am the Third Wave."

Third-wave feminism also traces its roots to the emergence of the riot grill feminist punk subculture in Olympia, Washington, in the early 1990s, blending feminism, punk music, and politics.

- Seeks to challenge or avoid what it deems the second wave's essentialist definitions of femininity (womanliness), which often overemphasize the experiences of upper-middle-class white women.

Issues that fourth-wave feminists focus on include:

- Street and workplace harassment, campus sexual assault, and rape culture.
- Scandals involving the harassment, abuse, and murder of women and girls have galvanized the movement. For example:
    - 2012 Delhi gang rape.
    - The 2012 Jimmy Savile allegations.
    - The Bill Cosby allegations.
    - The 2014 Isla Vista killings.

- The 2016 trial of Jian Ghomeshi.
- The 2017 Harvey Weinstein allegations.
- The 2017 Westminster sexual scandals.

The 2017 Women's March in Washington, D.C., was a worldwide protest the day after the inauguration of Donald Trump as US president. It was prompted by Trump's policy positions and rhetoric, which protesters called misogynistic (women-hating) or otherwise threatening to the rights of women.

The International Women's Strike, Paraná, Argentina, 2019, calling for an end to the country's growing poverty

Examples of the fourth-wave feminist campaigns include:

- The Everyday Sexism Project.
- No More Page 3.
- Stop Build Sexism – a campaign opposing the objectification of women in Bild-Zeitung, the most popular newspaper in Germany.
- Mattress Performance.
- 10 Hours of Walking in NYC as a Woman.
- #YesAllWomen.
- Free the Nipple.
- One Billion Rising.
- The 2018 Women's March.
- #MeToo Movement.

In December 2017, Time magazine chose several prominent female activists involved in the #MeToo Movement, dubbed "the silence breakers," as Person of the Year.

CHAPTER 4

FEMINISM HISTORY

The feminist movement formally began at the Seneca Falls Convention in 1848, where 300 women and men rallied for gender equality. Elizabeth Cady Stanton drafted the Seneca Falls Declaration, outlining the new movement's ideology and political strategies.

Outspoken political activist, writer, and social theorist Simone de Beauvoir wrote "*The Second Sex*" in 1949, a groundbreaking book credited with paving the way for modern feminism.

Pioneers of the movement include Mary Wollstonecraft, Susan B. Anthony, Alice Stone Blackwell, Elizabeth Cady Stanton, Emmeline Pankhurst, and Sojourner Truth.

France
In late 14th- and early 15th-century France, the first feminist philosopher, Christine de Pisan, challenged prevailing attitudes toward women with a bold call for female education.

French philosopher Simone de Beauvoir provided a Marxist solution and an individualistic view on many feminist questions with her book "*Le Deuxième Sexe*" (*The Second Sex*) in 1949. The book expressed feminists' sense of injustice.

Simone Veil (1927–2017), former French Minister of Health (1974–79), made access to contraceptive pills easier and legalized abortion (1974–75) – her greatest and most challenging achievement.

In France, women gained the right to vote only with The Provisional Government of the French Republic on April 21,

1944. The Consultative Assembly of Algiers' proposal on March 24, 1944, granted women full citizenship and the right to vote.

Britain

In Britain, suffragettes (right to voters) and suffragists (women right to voters) campaigned for women's voting rights. The Representation of the People Act in 1918 granted the vote to women over the age of 30 who owned property. In 1928, this was extended to all women over 21.

Emmeline Pankhurst was the most notable activist in England. Time named her one of the 100 Most Important People of the 20th Century, stating that "she shaped an idea of women for our time and shook society into a new pattern from which there could be no going back."

Switzerland

In Switzerland, women gained the right to vote in federal elections in 1971.

Liechtenstein

In Liechtenstein, women were granted the right to vote by the women's suffrage referendum of 1984, after three prior referendums in 1968, 1971, and 1973 had failed to secure women's voting rights.

USA

In the USA, notable leaders included Lucretia Mott, Elizabeth Cady Stanton and Susan B. Anthony initially campaigned for the abolition of slavery before championing women's right to vote. These women were influenced by Quaker theology, which asserted the spiritual equality of men and women.

The U.S. Department of State has prioritized advancing gender equality and the status of women and girls worldwide in various areas.

China

During the late Qing period and reform movements, Chinese feminists called for women's liberation from traditional roles and gender segregation. The Chinese Communist Party later aimed to integrate women into the workforce and claimed to have achieved women's liberation.

Arab Feminism

Arab feminism was closely connected with Arab nationalism. In 1899, Qasim Amin, considered the father of Arab feminism, wrote "*The Liberation of Women*," advocating for legal and social reforms. Hoda Shaarawi founded the Egyptian Feminist Union in 1923.

Iran

The Iranian women's movement began during the Iranian Constitutional Revolution in 1905. It aimed to achieve women's equality in education, marriage, careers, and legal rights. However, many of these gains were reversed during the Iranian revolution of 1979.

Latin America

In Latin America, revolutions brought changes in women's status in countries like Nicaragua. Feminist ideology during the
The Sandinista Revolution improved women's lives but fell short of achieving significant social and ideological change.

World Wars

During the baby boom period, feminism declined in importance. Both World War I and II saw the temporary liberation of women, but the post-war period signaled a return to conservative roles.

CHAPTER 5

PATRIARCHY

Patriarchy is a social system in which society is organized around male authority figures. In this system, fathers have authority over women, children, and property. It implies the institutions of male rule and privilege and is dependent on female subordination.

Husband Control
Feminists continued to campaign for the reform of family laws that gave husbands control over their wives. The 20th-century coverture (concealment) was a legal doctrine in English common law in which a married woman's legal existence was considered merged with that of her husband. She had no independent legal existence of her own.

It had been abolished in the UK and US, but in many Continental European countries, married women still had very few rights. For instance, in France, married women did not receive the right to work without their husband's permission until 1965.

Marital Exemption
Feminists have also worked to abolish the "marital exemption" in rape laws, which precluded the prosecution of husbands for the rape of their wives. Earlier efforts by first-wave feminists to criminalize marital rape in the late 19th century had failed. This was only achieved a century later in most Western countries but is still not achieved in many other parts of the world.

Sex Industry
Opinions on the sex industry are diverse. Feminists who are critical of the sex industry generally see it as the exploitative result of patriarchal social structures that reinforce sexual and cultural attitudes complicit (wrongful involvement) in rape and sexual harassment.

Alternatively, feminists who support at least part of the sex industry argue that it can be a medium of feminist expression and a means for women to take control of their sexuality. Feminist views of pornography range from condemnation of pornography as a form of violence against women to an embrace of some forms of pornography as a medium of feminist expression. Similarly, feminists' views on prostitution vary, ranging from critical to supportive.

Affirming Female Sexual Autonomy
For feminists, a woman's right to control her own sexuality is a key issue. Feminists such as Catharine MacKinnon argue that women have little control over their own bodies, with female sexuality being largely controlled and defined by men in patriarchal societies. Feminists argue that sexual violence committed by men is often rooted in ideologies of male sexual entitlement and that these systems grant women very few legitimate options to refuse sexual advances. Feminists argue that all cultures are, in one way or another, dominated by ideologies that largely deny women the right to decide how to express their sexuality because men under patriarchy feel entitled to define sex on their terms. This entitlement can take different forms depending on the culture.

In some conservative and religious cultures, marriage is regarded as an institution that requires a wife to be sexually available at all times, virtually without limit. Thus, forcing or coercing sex on a wife is not considered a crime or even abusive behavior. In more liberal cultures, this entitlement takes the form of a general sexualization of the whole culture. This is played out in the sexual objectification of women, with pornography and other forms of sexual entertainment creating the fantasy that all women exist solely for men's sexual pleasure and that women are readily available and desiring to engage in sex at any time, with any man, on a man's terms.

CHAPTER 6

RELIGION AND FEMINISM

Christian Feminism is a school of Christian theology that seeks to advance and understand the equality of men and women morally, socially, spiritually, and in leadership from a Christian perspective. Christian feminists argue that contributions by women and an acknowledgment of women's value are necessary for a complete understanding of Christianity. Christian feminists believe that God does not discriminate on the basis of biologically determined characteristics such as sex and race but created all humans to exist in harmony and equality, regardless of race or gender.

Christian feminists generally advocate for anti-essentialism as a part of their belief system, acknowledging that gender identities do not mandate a set of personality traits. Their major issues include the ordination (making religious leaders) of women, biblical equality in marriage, recognition of equal spiritual and moral abilities, abortion rights, integration of gender-neutral pronouns within readings of the Bible, and the search for a feminine or gender-transcendent divine. Christian feminists often draw on the teachings of other religions and ideologies in addition to biblical evidence and other Christian-based texts throughout history that advocate for women's rights.

Complementarianism is a theological view in Christianity, Judaism, and Islam that men and women have different but complementary roles and responsibilities in marriage, family life, and religious leadership.

There are a number of academic journals dedicated to promoting feminist theological scholarship. These include:
- Journal of Feminist Studies in Religion.
- Women-Church Journal (1988-2007).

- In God's image, produced by the Asian Women's Resource Centre for Culture and Theology.
- Feminist Theology.

Roman Catholicism

There have been Popes like Pope John Paul II and Pope Francis who have referenced a type of Feminism in their addresses to the public. Pope Francis is quoted saying the "irreplaceable role of the woman in the family... the gifts of delicacy... which are a richness of the feminine spirit, represent a genuine force for the life of the family... without which the human vocation would be unrealizable." Some men and women took Pope Francis' words as "vivid hope" that women will take a more prominent role in the Catholic Church.

On Wednesday, April 26, 2023, Pope Francis approved changes to the norms governing the Synod of Bishops, a Vatican body that gathers the world's bishops together for periodic meetings, following decades of demands by women to have the right to vote.

Buddhist Feminism

It is a movement that seeks to improve the religious, legal, and social status of women within Buddhism. It is an aspect of feminist theology that seeks to advance and understand the equality of men and women morally, socially, spiritually, and in leadership from a Buddhist perspective. The Buddhist feminist Rita Gross describes Buddhist feminism as the radical practice of the co-humanity of women and men.

Jewish Feminism

It is a movement that seeks to improve the religious, legal, and social status of women within Judaism and to open up new opportunities for religious experience and leadership for Jewish women. The main issues for early Jewish feminists in these movements were the exclusion from the all-male prayer group, the exemption from positive time-bound rules, and women's inability to function as witnesses and to initiate divorce. Many Jewish women have become leaders of feminist movements throughout their history.

Dianic Wicca / Dianic Witchcraft is a Modern Pagan goddess tradition focused on female experience and empowerment. Leadership is by women, who may be ordained as priestesses, or in less formal groups that function as collectives.

Secular Or Atheist Feminism
It has engaged in feminist criticism of religion, arguing that many religions have oppressive rules towards women and misogynistic themes and elements in religious texts.

CHAPTER 7

ISLAMIC FEMINISM

Islamic feminists advocate for women's rights, gender equality, and social justice grounded within an Islamic framework. They seek to highlight the deeply rooted teachings of equality in the Qur'an and encourage a questioning of patriarchal interpretations of Islamic teachings found in the Qur'an, the hadith (the sayings of Prophet Muhammad), and the Sharia (law). Their aim is to contribute to the creation of a more equal and just society. While rooted in Islam, the movement's pioneers have also drawn from secular and Western feminist discourses and recognize the role of Islamic feminism as part of an integrated global feminist movement.

According to the Qur'an:

> It is God Who created mankind from a single soul Adam and its mate Eve so that you may enjoy the pleasure of living with her. When you had sexual intercourse with her, she became pregnant and carried the child for a while when it was light. When it became heavy, you both prayed to God saying: If You (God) give us a good child, we shall be grateful. (7:189)

> ...The women have rights similar to the rights of men, but men have status over them.... (2:228)

A woman and a man are not biologically the same and have differing specific roles. A woman has a vagina and a uterus, while a man has a penis. In God's creation of mankind, both are essential. For example, a woman conceives a child, carries the child for 40 weeks in her body, delivers it, and raises it to be a man/woman. God has created a unique, unbreakable, lifelong bond of love between a mother and a child.

During pregnancy, a woman goes through complex and varying circumstances of life and death. During pregnancy, her husband is supposed to support her psychologically and physically and provide for her needs. This isn't a favor to her but rather his God-given responsibility as a husband and father. This is why God has given men a status of responsibility over women. This status involves the responsibility of making a family function as a team. In a family, the head of the family, the husband, the father, the wife, the mother, the son, the daughter, the brother, and the sister each have their individual status and responsibility. No one has supremacy over the other. They are all part of God's family team. This is how God has created humanity and mankind, without which God's universe would not have been complete and functional.

CHAPTER 8

ISLAMIC JUSTICE

It is an injustice to women not to allow them to:

- Vote.
- Run for public office.
- Work.
- Earn equal pay.
- Own property.
- Receive education.
- Enter contracts.
- End oppression.
- Protect against sexual harassment and assault.
- Have:

    o Reproductive rights.
    o Maternity leave.

This is what God has said about justice in the Qur'an:

> These are God's revelations. We recite them to you O Muhammad in truth. God wants no injustice to His creatures. (3:108)

> If you fear that you would not be able to treat orphan girls justly, then you may marry other women of your choice, two, three or four of them. But if you fear that you would not be able to treat them equally, marry only one or a slave girl you may own. That will be a better way to avoid injustice. (4:3)

> Believers do not consume one another's property unjustly; rather trade it by mutual consent. Do not kill one another. God has been most merciful to you. Whoever will commit such acts of aggression and injustice shall be thrown into hellfire. That is easy for God. (4:29-30)

God does not do injustice even of an atom's weight to anyone. If there is a good action, He multiplies it and gives a great reward from Himself. (4:40)

God does not forgive the worshipping of other gods besides Him. But forgives whom He pleases for other sins. He who associates anything with God has certainly fabricated a tremendous sin. Have you seen those who claim themselves to be pure? God purifies whom He wills. Injustice will not be done to them in the least. Look, how they invent lies about God. That of itself is a flagrant sin. (4:48-50)

If anyone does good deeds, whether male or female and has faith, will enter paradise, and the least injustice will be done to them. (4:124)

Those who believe and do not mix their belief with injustice will have salvation and are rightly guided. (6:82)

Record of their deeds will be placed before them on the Day of Judgment. You will see criminals fearful of its contents, saying: Woe to us! What kind of book is this that leaves out nothing; all small or great acts are written in it? They will find all their deeds recorded there. Your Lord will not do injustice to anyone. (18:49)

All faces will be humbled before God, the ever-living, and ever-sustaining. The sinner who carried injustice will have failed. (20:111)

The believer who acts rightly will neither fear injustice nor the loss of his reward. (20:112)

The disbelievers say: The Qur'an is a lie that Prophet Muhammad has forged with the assistance of others. In fact, it is the disbelievers who have committed an injustice and a lie. (25:4)

Then God will address the disbelievers: Your idols have proved you wrong. They can neither avert your punishment nor help you. Those of you who have committed injustice will be severely punished. (25:19)

That Day (of Judgement), every person shall be rewarded for what the person has earned. No injustice shall be done. God is quick in taking account. (40:17)

The person who was a believer said: My people, indeed I fear for you a fate like that of the earlier disbelievers, for example, the people of Noah, Aad and Thamoud, and those after them. God does not want to do any injustice to His servants. (40:30-31)

God abhors injustice and advises humans to work for justice diligently. The following is the summary of the above verses:

- God:

    o wants no injustice to His creatures.
    o does not do injustice even of an atom's weight to anyone.
    o will address the disbelievers: Your idols have proved you wrong. They can neither avert your punishment nor help you. Those of you who have committed injustice will be severely punished.

- If you fear that you would not be able to treat orphan girls justly, then you may marry other women of your choice, two, three or four of them. But if you fear that you would not be able to treat them equally, marry only one or a slave girl you may own. That will be a better way to avoid injustice.

- Believers:

    - do not consume one another's property unjustly; …. Whoever will commit such acts of aggression and injustice shall be thrown into the hellfire….
    - who acts rightly will neither fear injustice nor loss of his reward.

- …. Have you seen those who claim themselves to be pure? God purifies whom He wills. Injustice will not be done to them in the least. ….
- If anyone does good deeds, whether male or female and has faith, will enter paradise, and the least injustice will be done to them.
- Those who believe and do not mix their belief with injustice will have salvation and are rightly guided.
- Record of humans' deeds will be placed before them on the Day of Judgment. You will see criminals fearful of its contents, saying: Woe to us! What kind of book is this that leaves out nothing; all small or great acts are written in it? They will find all their deeds recorded there. Your Lord will not do injustice to anyone.
- …. The sinner who carried injustice will have failed.
- The disbelievers say: The Qur'an is a lie that Prophet Muhammad has forged with the assistance of others. In fact, it is the disbelievers who have committed an injustice and a lie.
- That Day of Judgment, every person shall be rewarded for what the person has earned. No injustice shall be done.
- The person who was a believer said: My people, indeed I fear for you a fate like that of the earlier disbelievers, for example, the people of Noah, Aad and Thamoud, and those after them. God does not want to do any injustice to His servants.

In Islam, justice is fundamental to the religion irrespective of gender.

CHAPTER 9

ISLAMIC RIGHTS
MARRIAGE AND DIVORCE

Marriage
Marriage is a formal union and a social and legal contract between two individuals that unites their lives legally, economically, and emotionally. It also gives legitimacy to sexual relations within the marriage.

About marriage, God has said in the Quran:

> It is God Who created you humankind from a single soul Adam, and then its mate Eve so that you may enjoy the pleasure of living with her. When you had sexual intercourse with her, she became pregnant and carried the child for a while when it was light. When it became heavy, you both prayed to God saying: If You give us a good child, we shall be grateful. (7:189)

> It is God Who created humans from water (human semen), made them related to each other through descent and marriage.... (25:54)

> How could you take dowry back while you both have sexual intercourse with each other and enter into a firm contract? (4:21)

> There will be no blame on men if you make an offer of marriage to women indirectly or hold it in your hearts. God knows what is on your mind. Neither you make a secret contract with them except in a lawful manner nor resolve the tie of marriage till the prescribed term is fulfilled. Know that God knows what is in your hearts, therefore fear Him..... (2:235)

Marriage is forbidden to your mothers, daughters, sisters, father's and mother's sisters, brother's and sister's daughters, foster mothers who suckled you, foster sisters who suckled with you, mothers-in-law, stepdaughters under your guardianship, who were born to your wives with whom you have sexual intercourse, but there is no sin on you in marrying their daughters if you have not had sexual intercourse with your wives [their mothers] and you want to leave them to marry their daughters, the wives of your sons by blood, and two sisters at the same time, except for what has already happened..... (4:23)

You are prohibited from marrying married women except the war-captive slave women you own. This is God's decree for you. All other women are lawful to you, provided you seek them in marriage by giving them dowry from your property, desire virtuous character and not unlawful sexual intercourse. To enjoy marriage with them, give them their obligatory dowry. However, there is no harm in consensual compromise for the dowry.... (4:24)

Whoever cannot afford to marry a free-believing woman, can marry a war-captive believing slave-girl he owns. God has full knowledge of your faith. You being from the same community, marry them with their guardian's permission and give them their fair dowries, provided they are virgins, have not committed unlawful intercourse, and do not have secret lovers. But once they are married, if they commit adultery, their punishment is half that of a free unmarried woman. This allowance is for those who fear committing sin, but self-control is better for you..... (4:25)

This day, the following have been made lawful for you:

- all things good and pure,

- the food of the People of the Book (Jews and Christians) and your food for them, and
- marriage to chaste women, both from believers and the People of the Book, when you give them their dowries, live in honor with them, do not commit fornication [sex between unmarried partners] and become their secret lovers. Whoever rejects faith, his labor will be fruitless. In the hereafter, he will be among the losers. (5:5)

Arrange marriages between single men and women among you and between virtuous male and female slaves. If they are poor, God will enrich them from His grace..... (24:32)

Those who find no means for marriage should stay away from sexual relations until God enriches them out of His grace. Free your slaves who want to buy their freedom, if they are trustworthy. Give them a part of your riches which God has given you. Do not force your slave girls into prostitution for you to earn money if they desire to keep themselves out of it. But if anyone would compel them, God will forgive the slave-girls and be merciful to them. (24:33)

Believers, when you marry believing women and then divorce them before you have intercourse with them, then there is no waiting period to complete the divorce. Provide for them and give them a gracious release. (33:49)

Believers, when the believing women come to you as emigrants, examine their faith. God best knows their faith. If you find them to be believers, do not return them to the disbelievers; they are neither lawful wives for them, nor are lawful husbands for them. But, give the disbelievers the dowries they gave them. There is no blame upon you if you marry them, provided you give them their dowries. Do not hold on to your marriage with the disbelieving women, but ask for the dowries you have given them and let the disbelievers do the same. That is God's decision....... (60:10)

For women who have passed the menstrual age and have no desire for marriage, there will be no offence to remove their cloaks without showing their adornments. However, it will be better if they do not remove their cloaks...... (24:60)

Test orphans' abilities until they reach a marriageable age. If you find them of sound judgment, hand over their property to them. Do not consume it excessively and quickly anticipating that they will grow up soon. Whoever is self-sufficient as a guardian, should refrain from taking a fee. Whoever is poor, should take what is reasonable. When you hand over their property, have witnessed in their presence..... (4:6)

Divorce
Divorce is a legal ending of a marriage granted by a court or another competent body. In Islam, divorce is of two types. Divorce initiated by the:

1. Husband
2. Wife

The husband can announce a divorce without going to court, but in the case of the wife, the matter has to be brought before a legal authority to protect her rights.

About divorce, God has said in the Quran:

There is a four-month waiting period for those (husbands) who swear not to have relations with their wives. But if they return to normal relations, God is forgiving and merciful. (2:226)

If the husbands have decided upon a divorce to the wives, know that God hears and knows everything. (2:227)

Divorced women shall wait for three menstruation periods. It is unlawful for them, if they have faith in God and the last day, to hide what God has created in their wombs. Their husbands have the right to take them back in that period if they wish for reconciliation. The women have rights similar to the rights of men, but men have status over them….. (2:228)

A divorce is only permissible twice. After that, the wife should either be retained honorably or let go with kindness. It is not lawful for men to take back anything they gave to their wives unless they both fear that they would be unable to keep the limits decreed by God. In that case, there will be no blame on either one of them if she would give something to be released from the marriage bond. These are the limits decreed by God. Do not cross them. Those who cross limits are the wrongdoers. (2:229)

If a husband divorces his wife for the third time, he cannot remarry her until she has married another husband, and that husband has divorced her. There is no harm if they remarry; provided the woman and her former husband think that they can keep the limits set by God. These are the limits set by God, which He makes clear to those who understand. (2:230)

When you divorce women and they have completed their waiting period, either take them back honorably or release them with kindness. But do not keep them to harass them. Whoever will do that would certainly wrong himself. Do not make a joke of God's verses….. (2:231)

When you divorce women and they complete their waiting period, do not prevent them from marrying their prospective husbands if they agree in a lawful manner. This instruction is for those who believe in God and the last day. This is more virtuous and purer for you.... (2:232)

There is no blame on you if you divorce women before touching them or fixing the dowry. However, give them a suitable gift, the wealthy according to his means, and the poor according to his means. This is an obligation upon the virtuous. (2:236)

If you divorce the women before touching, but after fixing the dowry, give them half of the dowry, unless they forgo it, or the husband forgoes his half as the marriage tie is in his hands. The forgoing of the man's half is closest to righteousness. Do not forget to show kindness to each other..... (2:237)

If you want to divorce one wife to wed another and you have given the former a great amount of dowry, do not take back anything from her. That would be improper and grossly unjust. (4:20)

How could you take it back while you both have sexual intercourse with each other and enter into a firm contract? (4:21)

Believers, when you marry believing women and then divorce them before you have intercourse with them, then there is no waiting period to complete the divorce. Provide for them and give them a gracious release. (33:49)

If you fear a breach between a husband and his wife, appoint an arbitrator from his family and another from her family. If they desire reconciliation, God will cause their reconciliation...... (4:35)

God created humanity through the marriage of Adam and Eve. In Islam, sexual relations are only permissible between a legally married man and woman. In the Quran, God has defined the conditions for permissible marriages. Dowry must be given to the wife and cannot be reclaimed in the event of divorce. Sexual relations outside of marriage are considered sinful in Islam. God punished the nation of Prophet Lot for engaging in same-sex relations.

In Islam, divorce is permissible, but the Prophet of Islam referred to it as the least desirable option in God's sight.

Just as marriage is a choice made by a man and a woman, so is divorce. There can be many reasons for divorce, but God advises that reconciliation through arbitration is preferable, provided both the wife and husband desire it. It is a matter of both the heart (love and compassion) and the mind. The divorcing couples are humans and can make mistakes. They should not rush into divorce and should reflect upon the potential negative consequences for their children, their families, friends, and society at large.

In Islam, there is a waiting period after divorce:

- Husbands have a four-month waiting period during which they must swear not to have relations with their wives. This prevents them from making impulsive decisions.
- Divorced women must wait for three menstruation periods. It is unlawful for them, if they have faith in God and the last day, to conceal what God has created in their wombs. During this period, their husbands have the right to take them back if they seek reconciliation. Women have rights similar to men, but men hold a higher status.

The purpose of the waiting period is to ensure that the wife is not pregnant. If she is, God encourages reconciliation for the well-being of the unborn child.

In the above verses, the following issues require clarification:

- Whoever cannot afford to marry a free-believing woman, can marry a war-captive believing slave-girl he owns. God has full knowledge of your faith. You being from the same community, marry them with their guardian's permission and give them their fair dowries, provided they are virgins, have not committed unlawful intercourse, and do not have secret lovers. But once they are married, if they commit adultery, their punishment is half that of a free unmarried woman. This allowance is for those who fear committing sin, but self-control is better for you..... (4:25)

  A free unmarried woman has two protections: 1. Of her family; 2. Of the husband upon marriage. The war captive believes the slave girl has no protection for her family because she left her family because of the war. She only has the protection of her husband upon marriage. Therefore, God has prescribed half punishment for the married slave girl.

- For women who have passed the menstrual age and have no desire for marriage, there will be no offence to remove their cloaks without showing their adornments. However, it will be better if they do not remove their cloaks...... (24:60)

  A cloak is a loose garment worn over clothing like an overcoat. It protects the wearer from the weather. For women, it protects them from men gazing at their body parts like breasts and buttocks.

God has given freedom of choice to the older women who have no desire for marriage but has advised them not to show off their adornments and it would be better for them to keep wearing the cloaks.

- The women have rights similar to the rights of men, but men have status over them.
- When you divorce women and they have completed their waiting period, either take them back honorably or release them with kindness. But do not keep them to harass them. Whoever will do that would certainly wrong himself. Do not make a joke of God's verses….. (2:231)

God has emphasized:

- o Taking divorced women back honorably or release with kindness.
- o Do not keep the divorced women to harass them.

CHAPTER 10

ABORTION IN ISLAM

Abortion is the deliberate termination of a human pregnancy. About abortion, God has said in the Quran:

> Do not kill your children for fear of poverty. We provide for them and you. Killing them is a great sin. (17:31)
>
> Do not commit adultery. It is immoral and evil. (17:32)
>
> Do not kill anyone because God has forbidden it, except for a just cause. If someone is killed unjustly, We have given his heir the right to demand justice. But let him not exceed limits in taking a life, as the victim has rights too. (17:33)
>
> O Prophet, if believing women come to you to take an oath of allegiance and pledge that they will not worship anyone but God, will not steal, commit adultery, kill their children, invent a lie, and disobey you for what is right, accept their oath and ask God to forgive them….. (60:12)

In summary, God has forbidden the following:

- Killing your children for fear of poverty, as He provides for them and you, and killing is a grave sin.
- Taking a life unjustly, except for a just cause.
- Committing adultery.

Adultery refers to voluntary sexual intercourse between a married person and someone who is not their spouse. It is considered objectionable on social, religious, moral, and legal grounds. While the specific acts that constitute adultery may vary, the social, religious, and legal consequences are similar in Judaism, Christianity, and Islam.

Some questions that arise are:

- What constitutes a just cause for taking the life of a child?
- At what point during pregnancy does a fetus become considered a child, at conception or at birth?
- Should a child be aborted due to the circumstances of adultery?"

These topics have been the subjects of theological, political, social, and medical debates for centuries. In my opinion:

- Many abortions are carried out due to fear of poverty. Parents often presume that having more children will increase their financial burden, leading them to decide on abortion.
- God prohibits the killing of children due to poverty because He is the provider. Humans make efforts to earn, provide, and survive, but poverty is not a justifiable reason to take the life of an unborn child.
- Another significant reason for abortion is when a woman conceives a child out of wedlock. Conceiving a child outside of marriage is not sanctioned by God and is considered unnatural, immoral, and illegal. However, the following are my thoughts:

All abortions should not be prohibited.

- If a mother's life is medically threatened by childbirth, priority should be given to the mother's life over that of the unborn child. Saving a mother's life is a justifiable reason for abortion.

- In cases of rape, women should be allowed to terminate the pregnancy.
- Under these unavoidable circumstances, abortion should be performed during the earliest stages of pregnancy."

CHAPTER 11

ISLAMIC PROPERTY DISTRIBUTION

A will is a legal declaration of a person's after-death wishes regarding the disposal of her/his property or estate.

In Islam, an individual can draft a will for up to one-third of their estate. The remaining two-thirds must be distributed in accordance with the shares defined in the Quran. In Islamic tradition, a will is executed after covering funeral expenses and settling outstanding debts. The person making the will is referred to as the testator.

About a will, God has stated in the Quran:

> When death approaches you, you should distribute your wealth by will equitably to your parents and relatives. This is a duty upon those who guard against evil. (2:180)
>
> It is sinful to alter the will after hearing it….. (2:181)
>
> If anyone suspects partiality or wrongdoing on the part of the person who left the will, and makes a settlement between the affected parties, there is no wrongdoing on his part….. (2:182)
>
> Those who die and leave widows behind should provide in their will a year's maintenance and residence for them. If they leave on their own, there will be no blame on you for what they do in an honorable way…… (2:240)
>
> Believers, when death approaches you and you make

a will, take two just men among you as witnesses, or two outsiders even non-Muslims if you are traveling through the land and death strikes you. If you doubt their honesty, stop them after prayer, and let them swear by God saying: We will not exchange our oath for a price, even for a near relative, and we will not withhold testimony which we are giving for the sake of God, otherwise, we would be sinful. (5:106)

If it is found that those two lied under oath, let two others from those who are trustworthy and have a lawful right to represent the affected parties stand in their place. Let them swear by God: Our testimony is truer than their testimony, and we have not exceeded the limits of our duty, otherwise, we would be wrongdoers. (5:107)

God's orders for the distribution of your inheritance are:

- For children, a male's share will be twice of a female.
- If daughters only then they have two or more, their share is two-thirds. If one daughter only, her share is half.
- For parents, each has a sixth share if the deceased left children. If there are no children and the parents are the only heirs, the mother has a third. If the deceased left brothers or sisters, the mother has a sixth.
- The above distributions shall be after complying with the deceased's will and paying her/his debts.
- You do not know whether your parents or children are more beneficial to you. But these are God's orders..... And:
- Your share is half of what your wives leave if they leave no child. But if they leave a child, you get a fourth.
- Your wives' share is a fourth of what you leave, if you leave no child. But if you leave a child, they get an eighth.
- If the deceased has left neither parents nor children but

has left a brother or a sister, each one gets a sixth. But if there are more than two, their share is a third.
- The above distributions shall be after complying with the deceased's will and paying her/his debts provided no loss is caused to anyone.
- The distribution is ordered by God….. (4:11-12)

CHAPTER 12

ISLAMIC DEBT

Debt is an obligation that necessitates one party, the debtor, to pay money or another agreed-upon value to another party, the creditor. Debt involves deferred payment or a series of payments, setting it apart from an immediate purchase.

About debt, God has said in the Quran:

> Believers, when you take a debt for a specified period, write it down. Let a scribe write it justly. No scribe should refuse to write it as God has given him the gift of writing. So let him write and the debtor dictates, fearing God and leaving nothing out of it. But if the debtor is of limited understanding or is weak or unable to dictate himself, let his guardian dictate for him justly. Get two male witnesses; if not available, select a man and two women from those whom you consider suitable witnesses. If either woman would err, the other would remind her. Witnesses should not refuse to witness when called upon to do so. Do not fail to write whether it is a small or a large debt with its specified term. That is more just in God's sight, ensures accuracy in evidence, and prevents doubts. However, if it is an on-the-spot transaction, there is no blame upon you if you do not write it. But take witnesses when you conclude a contract. No scribe or witness should be harmed. If you will do so, you will commit a sin..... (2:282)

> If you are on a journey and cannot find a scribe, then a security deposit should be taken. If one of you entrusts another, then let the trustee discharge his trust-fearing God, her/his Lord. Do not conceal testimony. Whoever conceals it, her/his heart is

sinful..... (2:283)

The charitable donations shall be used only for the poor, needy, debtors, collectors of charity, and converts to Islam, freeing slaves, God's cause, and travelers. This is an obligation decided by God..... (9:60)

Are you [O Muhammad] asking them [the disbelievers] for a payment that they are afraid to be burdened with debt? (52:40)

If We (God) willed, we could turn the crops into chaff for you to wonder and say: We are burdened with debt and are ruined. (56:65–67)

In summary:

- When you take a debt with its specified term, write it down.
- A scribe should not refuse to write down the debt and should write it justly.
- No scribe or witness should be harmed.
- If the debtor is of limited understanding or is weak or unable to dictate himself/herself, let the guardian dictate for the debtor justly.
- Get two male witnesses; if not available, select a man and two women from those whom you consider suitable witnesses.
- Witnesses should not refuse to witness.
- Do not conceal testimony.
- For an on-the-spot transaction, there is no blame upon you, the debtor, if you do not write it. But take witnesses when you conclude a contract.
- If you are on a journey and cannot find a scribe, then a security deposit should be taken.
- Make distribution of your inheritance after paying the debts.
- Charitable donations can be used for the debtor.

It is noteworthy that God emphasizes that when a person dies, their debt should be settled before the distribution of their inheritance. Furthermore, when spending in God's way, one should not fear becoming impoverished. It is said that some companions of Prophet Muhammad even incurred debt to help protect the community from its enemies.

CHAPTER 13

WOMEN IN ISLAM

Women are adult females.

According to the Quran, God first created Adam, a man, and then Eve, the first woman, as his wife. From them, God created all of humankind.

> O mankind, fear your Lord, Who created you from a single person [Adam] and created, of like nature [human], his wife [Eve], and from both spread many men and women on earth. Fear God, in Whose name you claim the rights from one another and avoid violating the ties of the relationship. God is ever watching over you. (4:1)

> It is God Who created you [humankind] from a single soul, and then its mate so that you may enjoy the pleasure of living with her. When you had sexual intercourse with her, she became pregnant and carried the child for a while when it was light. When it became heavy, you both prayed to God saying: If You give us a good child, we shall be grateful. (7:189)

In this chapter, the following topics related to women are discussed:

- Exemplary Women
- Veil
- Dowry
- Menstruation
- Abortion
- Widowhood

Exemplary Women

Exemplary means a desirable model, representing the best of its kind.

Chapter 4 of the Quran is titled Women. The chapter includes topics related to women: treatment, justice, number of wives, dowry, punishment of illegal sexual relations, types of women prohibited from marriage, marriage with slave girls, corrective measures for disobedient women, and arbitration in family disputes. In addition, God gave examples of women in the Quran:

- Pharaoh's wife.
- Imran's daughter, Maryam (Mary), mother of Prophet Jesus.
- Wives of Prophets Noah and Lot, the Egyptians who bought Joseph, and Abu Lahab.

God would like believers to follow Pharaoh's wife and Mary but not the other three.

About exemplary women, God has said in the Quran:

> Pharaoh's wife said to him: He [Moses as a child] would bring us joy. Do not kill him. He may benefit us, or we may adopt him as a son. They did not know what they were doing. (28:9)

> For the believers, God cites an example of Pharaoh's wife, who said: Lord, build me a house in Your paradise and save me from Pharaoh, his sins, and the wrongdoing people. (66:11)
> Remember when Imran's wife said: Lord, I dedicate the child in my womb to Your service. Accept it from me. ….. (3:35)

> When she [Imran's wife] delivered the baby, she said: Lord, I have delivered a girl. God knew what she had

delivered. The male is not like the female; I have named her Mary; protect her and her descendants from Satan, the outcast. (3:36)

God graciously accepted her [Mary], made her grow in a good manner, and put her in Zechariah's care. Whenever he visited her in her chamber, he found food with her. He asked: Mary, where does this food come from? She replied: This is from God. He provides to whom He wills without limit. (3:37)

Another cited example is of Mary [Mother of Jesus], Imran's daughter, who guarded her virginity. We breathed into her Our spirit. She trusted the words of her Lord and His books. She was a pious servant. (66:12)

For the disbelievers, God cites an example of Noah's wife and Lot's wife. They were married to two of Our righteous servants but betrayed them. Their husbands could not protect them from God. Both were told to enter the fire with others. (66:10)

The angels said: O Lot, we are your Lord's messengers. Your enemies will not be able to touch you. Leave with your family, except your wife, during the remaining portion of the night, and no one should look back. Your wife will be punished by others. They will be punished in the morning. .... (11:81)

The Egyptian who bought Joseph said to his wife: Treat him nicely. He may prove useful for us, or we may adopt him as a son. Thus, We established Joseph in the land and taught him the interpretation of mysteries. God is the master of His affairs, but most people do not know it. (12:21)

His [Joseph's] master's wife tried to seduce him. She closed the doors and said: Come. He replied: God protect me. Your husband, my master, has been kind to me. The wrongdoers never succeed. (12:23.)

She [the wife of Joseph's master] said: That is the one about whom you blamed me. I certainly tried to seduce him, but he refused. If he will not do what I order him, he will be imprisoned and disgraced. (12:32)

The king asked the women: What took place when you tried to seduce Joseph? They replied: God forbid, we know no evil about him. The wife of the noble said: Now, the truth has come out. It was I who tried to seduce him, but he has told the truth. (12:51)

Abu Lahab and his wife were diehard opponents of Prophet Muhammad. He was the Prophet's neighbor and an uncle. Abu Lahab's wife used to throw thorns and trash where Prophet Muhammad would walk. In chapter 111 of the Quran, God has said:

May the hands of Abu Lahab perish, and may he perish. His wealth and what he has earned will not benefit him. He shall soon burn in a flaming fire, and his wife, the carrier of firewood, shall have a rope of palm-fibers around her neck. (111:1–5)

Prophet Muhammad's daughters, Ruqaiya and Umm Kulthum, were married to sons of Abu Lahab, but the marriages were never consummated (had sex). Under pressure from their father, both sons divorced Prophet Muhammad's daughters. The reason was Abu Lahab's hatred for Islam.

Veil

A veil is a cloth worn by women to conceal the face. About the veil, God has said in the Quran:

O Prophet, tell the believing men to lower their gaze and protect their private parts. That will purify them.

God is aware of what they do. (24:30)

O Prophet, tell the believing women:

- to lower their gaze,
- to protect their private parts,
- not to show off their adornments except what is normally visible,
- to draw their head covers on their chests, and
- not to display their adornment except to their:

  - husbands,
  - fathers,
  - father-in-laws,
  - sons,
  - step-sons,
  - brothers,
  - brother's sons,
  - sister's sons,
  - sisters in Islam,
  - slave-girls, and
  - male servants who lack sexual desire and children
  - who have no knowledge of a woman's private parts.

In addition, they should not stamp their feet while walking to reveal their hidden adornments. O believers, turn to God for forgiveness so that you may be successful. (24:31)

There is no blame on the Prophet's wives for appearing without a veil before:

- their fathers,
- sons,
- brothers,
- brother's sons,
- sisters' sons,
- familiar women, and

- slave-girls

Ladies, fear God, He observes all things. (33:55)

O Prophet, tell your wives, daughters, and believing women to bring down a part of their outer garment over their faces. That is more suitable for their recognition and to avoid lustful gaze. God is forgiving and merciful. (33:59)

Ladies with modest gaze will be in the gardens, whom neither a man nor jinn will have touched before. (55:56)

The objective of a veil is to cover ladies' faces and chests to avoid lustful gazes between men and women. It is a sign of modesty and piety. It avoids the start of illicit relations and prevents secret meetings between men and women. Not using the veil may lead to blaming and the breakup of a marriage.

Dowry

The dowry is the property settled between the wife and the husband at the time of marriage, which remains under her ownership and control.

In Islam, dowry is an obligatory payment in money or anything agreed upon by the bride, such as jewelry, home goods, furniture, a dwelling, or some land. In Islam, the dowry is one of the rights of the wife, which is hers to take in total and is lawful for her, in contrast to the widespread practice in some countries, where the wife is given no dowry.

About dowry, God has said in the Quran:

There is no blame on you if you divorce women before touching them or fixing the dowry. However, give them a suitable gift, the wealthy according to his means, and the poor according to his means. This is an obligation upon the virtuous. (2:236)

If you divorce them before touching, but after fixing the dowry, give them half of the dowry, unless they forgo it, or the husband forgoes his half as the marriage tie is in his hands. The forgoing of the man's half is closest to righteousness. Do not forget to show kindness to each other. God sees all your deeds. (2:237)

Give women their dowry willingly. But if they give you back some of it on their own, take it as lawfully yours. (4:4)

Believers, it is not lawful for you to inherit the widows of your deceased relative against their will. You should not treat them harshly in order to take back part of the dowry you gave them. If they committed adultery, punish them. Live with them in kindness. If you dislike them, it is possible that you dislike a thing and God brings you a lot of good through it. (4:19)

If you want to divorce one wife to wed another and you have given the former a great amount of dowry, do not take back anything from her. That would be improper and grossly unjust. (4:20)

You are prohibited from marrying married women except the war-captive slave women you own. This is God's decree for you. All other women are lawful to you, provided you seek them in marriage by giving them dowry from your property, desire virtuous character and not unlawful sexual intercourse. To enjoy marriage with them, give them their obligatory dowry. However, there is no harm in consensual compromise for the dowry. God is the ever-knowing and wise. (4:24)

Islam revolutionized women's rights and economics by making dowry obligatory. It is a lawful right of a woman, which is distributed to her heirs.

Menstruation

Is:

- the periodic shedding of the lining of a woman's uterus. The uterine lining breaks down into a bloody substance. It then passes down through the cervix and exits through the vagina. The process usually lasts from three to five days, at intervals of about one lunar month, from puberty until menopause, except during pregnancy.
- It is generally considered to be complete when a woman has not had a menstruation period for one year. Menopause, often referred to as the change of life, usually occurs between the ages of 45-55 years.

About menstruation, God has said in the Quran:

> They ask you about menstruation. Say: It is an unclean state; keep away from women during it, and do not approach them for sex until they are clean. Then you may approach them as God has prescribed for you. God loves those who turn to Him in repentance and keep themselves clean. (2:222)

> Divorced women shall wait for three menstruation periods. It is unlawful for them, if they have faith in God and the last day [of Judgment]; to hide what God has created in their wombs. Their husbands have the right to take them back in that period if they wish for reconciliation. The women have rights similar to the rights of men, but men have status over them. God is powerful and wise. (2:228)

> For women who have passed the menstrual age and have no desire for marriage, there will be no offence to remove their cloaks without showing their adornments. However, it will be better if they do not remove their cloaks. God hears all and knows all.

(24:60)

> If you are in doubt about the women who have passed the menstruation age, their waiting period is three months. For those who are pregnant, their period is until they give birth. God will ease the hardship of whoever fears Him. (65:4)

To ensure that the divorced woman is not pregnant, there is a waiting period of three menstrual cycles. For women who have passed the age of menstruation, their waiting period is three months. If she is pregnant, God encourages reconciliation for the welfare of the unborn child. Additionally, during the menstrual period, women are prohibited from going to a mosque for prayer, touching the Quran, or fasting during Ramadan.

Widowhood
A widow is a woman whose husband has died. In societies where the husband is the sole provider, his death can leave his family destitute (lacking necessities of life). The tendency for women, generally, to outlive men can compound this issue, as men in many societies often marry women younger than themselves. Islam provides a dowry for the economic welfare of the widow.

About widows, God has said in the Quran:

> After the husband's death, the widows shall keep away from men for four months and ten days. When they have fulfilled their term, there is no blame on you for what they do with themselves in an honorable manner. God is well aware of what you do. (2:234)

> Those who die and leave widows behind should provide in their will a year's maintenance and residence for them. If they leave on their own, there will be no blame on you for what they do in an honorable way. God is powerful and wise. (2:240)

Believers, it is not lawful for you to inherit the widows of your deceased relative against their will. You should not treat them harshly in order to take back part of the dowry you gave them. If they committed adultery, punish them. Live with them in kindness. If you dislike them, it is possible that you dislike a thing and God brings you a lot of good through it. (4:19)

Men are managers of women's affairs, because God has made men to excel women, and men spend their wealth to support the women. The righteous women are obedient. They guard men's rights in their absence because God wants them to guard those rights. As for those [women], you fear disloyalty and ill-conduct, advise them first, next refuse to share their beds, and lastly beat them lightly. If they return to obedience, take no further action against them. God is most high and great. (4:34)

The reason that, after the husband's death, the widow must refrain from interacting with men for four months and ten days is to ascertain whether she is pregnant. In such a case, her family should provide for both her and the child. Her dowry should not be taken away from her by the relatives of the deceased husband. That would be an additional injustice on top of losing her husband, especially when she is already distraught.

Marriage is a voluntary choice. Islam prohibits marrying widows against their will. They should not engage in adultery and should face punishment similar to other women who engage in illicit relations, disloyalty, or misconduct.

CHAPTER 14

SEX IN ISLAM

CHASTITY, INTERCOURSE, ADULTERY, FORNICATION, HOMOSEXUALITY

Sex refers to physical intimacy between a male and a female.

Chastity is the practice of refraining from extramarital sexual intercourse.

Sexual intercourse is the physical act of sex between two individuals.

Adultery is the voluntary engagement in sexual intercourse by a married person with someone who is not her/his spouse.

Fornication is sexual intercourse between unmarried individuals.

Homosexuality involves romantic attraction, sexual attraction, or sexual behavior between members of the same gender.

In the Quran, God has provided guidance about matters related to sex, including chastity, sexual intercourse, adultery, fornication, and homosexuality.

Chastity
This day, the following have been made lawful for you:

- all things good and pure,
- the food of the People of the Book [Jews and Christians] and your food for them, and
- marriage to chaste women, both from believers and the people of the book, when you give them their dowries, live in honor with them, do not commit fornication (sex between unmarried partners) and become their secret lovers. ... (5:5)

- Abstain from sexual relations. (23:5)
- Prophet Muhammad told the believing men to lower their gaze and protect their private parts. That will purify them. God is aware of what they do. (24:30)
- Prophet Muhammad told the believing women:

  - to lower their gaze,
  - to protect their private parts,
  - not to show off their adornments except what is normally visible,
  - to draw their head covers on their chests, and
  - not to display their adornment (for enhancing beauty) except to their:

    - husbands,
    - fathers,
    - father-in-laws,
    - sons,
    - step-sons,
    - brothers,
    - brother's sons,
    - sister's sons,
    - sisters in Islam,
    - slave-girls, and
    - male servants who lack sexual desire and children who have no knowledge of women's private parts.

  In addition, they should not stamp their feet while walking to reveal their hidden adornments. O believers, turn to God for forgiveness so that you may be successful. (24:31)
- God will forgive and reward both men and women who:

  - submit to God,
  - are believers, obedient, truthful, patient, and humble, and

- give charity, fast, guard their private parts, and remember God often. (33:35)

- And those who guard against their sexual desires, except their wives or the slave girls they possess, because they are lawful to them. (70:29-30)

Examples of Chastity
God has given examples of chastity in the Qur'an:

The wife of Prophet Joseph's master tried to seduce him. She closed the doors and said: Come. He replied: God protect me. Your husband, my master, has been kind to me. The wrongdoers never succeed. (12:23)

She certainly was determined to seduce him, and he would have been seduced had he not seen his Lord's sign. We warded off evil and immorality from him as he was one of Our chosen servants. (12:24)

Mary, mother of Jesus, said: How can I give birth to a child when I am a virgin and no man has touched me? (19:20)

O Aaron's sister*, your father was not adulterous, and your mother was not a prostitute. (19:28)

> *Aaron was a prophet. "O Aaron's sister" is not literal but is a "virtuous woman."*

Another cited example is of the Mother of Jesus, Imran's daughter, who guarded her virginity. We breathed into her Our spirit. She trusted the words of her Lord and His books. She was a pious servant. (66:12)

Sexual Intercourse Prohibition Between Married Couples
Per the Qur'an:

The months of pilgrimage are known. If one decides to perform the pilgrimage, he should abstain from sexual intercourse, obscenity, and quarrelling during these months. God knows whatever good you do. Take provisions for the pilgrimage journey, but the best provision is the right conduct. Fear Me O men of understanding. (2:197)

On nights during the fasting month, sexual intercourse with your wives is permitted. They are your garments, and you are their garments. God knew that you were deceiving yourselves. He has pardoned you and has removed this burden from you. Now you can associate with them, and seek what God has decreed for you. Eat and drink until you can distinguish between a white thread and a black thread in the light of the dawn; then complete your fast till the night appears. Do not associate with your wives while you are in retreat in the mosques. Those are limits set by God, so do not break them. God makes clear his signs to men that they may learn self-restraint. (2:187)

The men ask you Prophet Muhammad about menstruation. Say: It is an unclean state; keep away from women during it; and do not approach them for sex until they are clean. Then you may approach them as God has prescribed for you. God loves those who turn to Him in repentance and keep themselves clean. (2:222)

Believers, when you get ready for prayer, wash your faces, hands and arms to the elbows, wipe your heads, and wash your feet to the ankles. If you had sex, take a bath. But if you are ill, or on a journey, or have answered nature's call, or have been in sexual contact with women, and do not find water, take clean soil, and rub it on your faces and hands. God does not wish to burden you, but to make you clean and to complete his favor on you, so that you may be grateful. (5:6)

Adultery, Fornication, Homosexuality
Per the Qur'an:

> Successful are the believers, who are humble in their prayer, avoid profane talk, pay zakat [mandatory charity], abstain from sexual relations, outside their marriages with free women or slave girls. For that, there is no blame on them. (23:1–6)

> An adulterer may marry only an adulterous or an idolatress, and an adulterous may marry only an adulterer or an idolater. Such marriages are forbidden to the believers. (24:3)

> If any of your women commit illegal sexual intercourse, take the evidence of four witnesses from among you against them. If they testify to the allegation's truth, confine them to their houses until they die or God finds another way for them. (4:15)

Accusing Chaste Women of Adultery
According to the Qur'an:

> A hundred lashes should be given to an adulterer and an adulteress. No pity for them should make you disobey God, if you believe in God and the Last Day [of Judgment]. And let the believers witness their punishment. (24:2)

> Give 80 lashes to those who accuse honorable women without bringing out four witnesses, and never ever accept their testimony. They indeed are evildoers. Except those who repent and mend their ways. God is forgiving and merciful. If a man accuses his wife of adultery but has no witness, he should testify four times in God's name that he is telling the truth. He should testify a fifth time for God's curse to be on him should he be lying. She will not be punished if she testifies four times in God's name that her husband was lying. Her fifth

testimony should be for God's wrath to be upon her if she was lying. (24:4–9)

Prophet Lot's people, who were used to doing bad [sexual] acts, rushed to him. He said: O my people, these are my daughters, more lawful for you to marry. So fear God and do not disgrace me concerning my guests. Is there not a thoughtful man among you? (11:78)

They demanded from Lot his [angel] guests [to have sex with them], but We blinded their eyes and said: Taste My punishment when you have been warned. (54:37)

According to the above verses, during pilgrimage/hajj, one should abstain from sexual intercourse, obscenity, and quarreling. On nights during the fasting month, sexual intercourse with wives is permitted. Menstruation is an unclean state; one should keep away from women during it and not approach them for sex until they are clean.

Extramarital sex is considered objectionable on social, religious, moral, and legal grounds. God has mandated the following:

- A hundred lashes should be given to an adulterer and an adulteress. Do not let pity for them sway you in the matter of God's decree if you truly believe in God and the last day. Let the believers witness their punishment.

- If a woman commits illegal sexual intercourse, take the evidence of four witnesses. If they testify to the truth of the accusation, confine her to her house until her death or until God provides another way for her.

Believers should not offer prayers while in an unclean state due to a sexual discharge unless they have taken a bath. However, exceptions apply when they are traveling, sick, answering nature's call, or have had sexual contact with women and cannot find water. In such cases, they should take clean soil and wipe it over their faces and hands.

CHAPTER 15

USA FEMINISM GOAL

The goal of feminism in the USA is to challenge the systemic inequalities women face on a daily basis. It campaigns for women's rights to:

- Vote.
- Run for public office.
- Work.
- Earn equal pay.
- Own property.
- Receive education.
- Enter contracts.
- End oppression.
- Achieve gender equality in law and in practice.
- Protection against sexual harassment and assault.
- Have:

    - Reproductive rights.
    - Equal rights within marriage.
    - Maternity leave.

I support women's goals and campaigns, including achieving gender equality in both law and practice and equal rights within marriage. Women have made significant progress. They can:

- Vote.
- Run for public office.
- Work.
- Earn equal pay.
- Own property.
- Receive education.
- Enter contracts.

However, there's still work to be done to end women's oppression, protect them against sexual harassment and assault, ensure reproductive rights, and provide maternity leave.

I am 83 years old, a U.S. citizen for 48 years since 1976, of Pakistani heritage. I consider the USA a nation blessed by God. The USA has:

A political system with two main parties, the Republican Party and the Democratic Party

A system of checks and balances through its judiciary

The Republican Party often aligns with the interests of the wealthy and businessmen, while the Democratic Party focuses on the common people who are busy making a living.

The last president from the Republican Party was Trump, a businessman. The USA experimented with his leadership. You may want to read the latest books about him.

- Maggie Haberman, 2022 - *Confidence Man*.
- Peter Baker and Susan Glasser, 2022 - *The Divider*.
- Jonathan Karl, 2021- *Betrayal: The Final Act Of The Trump Show*.
- Jonathan Karl, 2020 - *Front Row At The Trump Show*.
- Mary L. Trump PhD, 2022 - *Too Much and Never Enough: How My Family Created the World's Most Dangerous Man*.

President Trump lost the last presidential election in 2020 but has not admitted it. His followers are mostly white, wealthy, and from rural areas. He is running again for the presidency in 2024 and has polarized the country. On January 6, 2022, his followers attacked the U.S. Congress in an attempt to stop the declaration of Joe Biden as the winner of the previous presidential election.

A U.S. House of Representatives committee has investigated the insurrection at the U.S. Capitol and President Trump's role in it.

President Trump's political strength was tested due to the results of the Mid-Term U.S. Congress elections on November 8, 2022. Few of his Republican candidates won.

Roe v. Wade, a landmark decision of the U.S. Supreme Court in 1973, recognized the constitutional right for women to have an abortion. However, on June 24, 2022, the current U.S. Supreme Court overturned Roe v. Wade, leaving the decision to the state legislatures.

The current Supreme Court comprises six conservative justices appointed by Republican Presidents and three liberal justices appointed by Democratic Presidents. Trump nominated three of the five conservative Supreme Court justices who voted to overturn Roe v. Wade.

The United States is one of the oldest modern democracies with a written constitution, and the fight for women's abortion rights will continue.

CHAPTER 16

FEMISISM OF DR. IQBAL

1877-1938

Sir Dr. Muhammad Iqbal was a South Asian Muslim writer, poet, philosopher, scholar, and politician. His poetry in the Urdu language is considered among the greatest of the twentieth century. His vision of a cultural and political ideal for the Muslims of British Rule was to animate (give life) the impulse for Pakistan. He is also known as Allama Iqbal, the National Poet of Pakistan.

The following are his nine poems about women:

Woman
To solve this riddle thinkers have much tried,
Their efforts all so far it has defied (failed).

No doubt, to woman's faith and conduct clear,
The Pleiades* and moon do witness bear.

a group of stars that is one of the nearest to Earth.

This vice in Frankish way of life (German invaders of western Europe in 5th century) we find,
Men fools and blind, can't read a woman's mind.

A Question
Ask the wise men of Europe, who have hung
Their ring in the nose of Greece and Hindustan:

Is this their civilization's highest rung—
A childless woman and a jobless man?

Veil
Great change the lofty spheres have met,
O God! The world has not budged as yet.

In man and wife is no contrast,
They like seclusion and hold it fast.

The sons of Adam still wear the mask,
But self hasn't peeped out of the casque (helmet).

Solitude
Much greed for show and fame has put this age to shame:
The glance is bright and clear, heart's mirror, but is blear (watery).

When zeal and zest for sight exceed their greatest height,
Thoughts soar to highest point and soon are out of joint.

That vernal (spring) drop of rain the state of pearl can't gain
If destined not to dwell, in lap of mother shell.

Retreat is blessed state about self gives knowledge great:
Alas! This state divine, isn't found in fane or shrine.

Woman
The picture that this world presents of a woman is: She is the lyre (stringed instrument) that can impart pathos (sadness) and warmth to human heart.

Her handful clay is superior far to Pleiades (a bright cluster of stars) that so higher are

For every man with knowledge vast, like gem out of her cask (barrel) is cast.

Like Plato cannot hold discourse, nor can with thunderous voice declaim:
But Plato was a spark that broke from her fire that blazed like a flame.

Emancipation Of Women
I know quite well that one despoils, while the other is like candy sweet:
I cannot give a verdict true which needs of quest (search) can fully meet.

I like to make no more remarks and earn the wrath of the present age:
Already the sons of the modern cult against me are full of ire and rage.

The insight owned by a woman can this subtle point with ease reveal:
Constrained and helpless, wise and sage, with knotty points they can not deal.

It is an uphill task to judge what is more precious, lends much grace:

Emancipation for fair sex or aught (nothing), or emerald-wrought superb neck-lace?

Protection Of The Women
A fact alive is in my breast concealed,
He can behold whose blood is not congealed (thickened).

To wear a veil and learn new lore or old,
Can't guard fair sex except a person bold.

A nation which can't see this truth divine,
Pale grows its son and soon begins decline.

Women And Education

If Frankish culture blights the motherly urge,
For human race it means a funeral dirge (song).

The lore that makes a woman lose her rank
Is naught but death in eyes of wise and frank.

If schools for girls no lore impart on creed,
Then lore and crafts for Love are death indeed.

Woman

The spirit of man can display its self without obligation to another,
But the spirit of woman cannot fully reveal it's self without another's help.

Her desire is the secret of her fever of sorrow:
Her existence is full of fire with the wish to create.

Here is the fire which opens the secrets of life;
That is the heat which sustains the struggle between to be and not to be.

I too feel sad about the oppression of women,
But this knotty problem cannot be resolved.

Summary

- Men can't read a woman's mind.
- A husband and wife have differing body structures and roles.
- A woman is a lyre (stringed instrument) that can impart pathos (sadness) and warmth to a human heart.
- Her handful of clay is superior far to Pleiades (a bright cluster of stars) that so higher are for every man with knowledge vast like gem out of her cask (barrel) is cast.
- The likes of the Greek philosopher Plato were born by women.

- The women own great insight, but are constrained and helpless, wise and sage, but cannot deal with their non-freedom in all spheres of life.
- It is an uphill task to judge what is more precious, lends much grace: Emancipation for fair sex or aught (nothing), or emerald-wrought superb neck-lace?
- A nation that can't protect its women soon begins to decline.
- If schools do not educate girls, then lore (knowledge) and crafts for love are indeed death.
- The spirit of man can display itself without obligation to another, But the spirit of woman cannot fully reveal itself without another's help. Teamwork is necessary.
- Her desire is the secret of her fever of sorrow: Her existence is full of fire with the wish to create.
- Here is the fire that opens the secrets of life; that is the heat that sustains the struggle between to be and not to be.
- I (Dr. Iqbal), too, feel sad about the oppression of women, but this knotty problem cannot be resolved.

CHAPTER 17

PROGRESS

In Time Magazine of April 29, 2024, list of The 100 Most Influential People Of The World includes 49 women out of 100:

- Artists – 7 out of 16
- Titans – 8 out of 15
- Leaders – 10 out of 24
- Innovators – 9 out of 15
- Icons – 9 out of 16
- Pioneers – 8 out of 14

In Time Magazine of May 13, 2024, list of The 100 Health Experts Of The World includes 40 women out of 100:

- Pioneers – 5 out of 20
- Leaders – 13 out of 21
- Catalysts – 11 out of 19
- Innovators – 8 out of 20
- Titans – 3 out of 20

CHAPTER 18

CONCLUSION

By gender, a woman is a female, and a man is a male. Their body structures and functions have distinctions.

A woman has a vagina and uterus, enabling her to conceive a child, carry the child in her abdomen for nine months, give birth, and breastfeed, nurturing the child's growth from infancy to adulthood.

A man has a penis, allowing him to engage in sexual intercourse with a woman to impregnate her. He is expected to support her during pregnancy and help educate their child to become successful, wealthy, and happy.

According to Islam's holy book, women and men have rights, but these rights are not equal or identical.

> ….. The women have rights similar to the rights of men, but men have status over them….. (2:228)

Men are managers of women's affairs, because God has made men to excel women, and men spend their wealth to support the women. The righteous women are obedient. They guard men's rights in their absence because God wants them to guard those rights. As for those [women], you fear disloyalty and ill-conduct, advise them first, next refuse to share their beds, and lastly beat them lightly. If they return to obedience, take no further action against them. God is most high and great. (4:34)

The similarity of the rights between women and men is for women to:

- Vote.

- Run for public office.
- Work.
- Earn equal pay.
- Own property.
- Receive education.
- Enter contracts.
- End oppression.
- Achieve gender equality in law and in practice.
- Protection against sexual harassment and assault.
- Have:

    - Reproductive rights.
    - Equal rights within marriage.
    - Maternity leave.

Islam has mandated the above rights in Islam's holy book. For example:

Dowry

Per the Qur'an:

> …. All other women are lawful to you, provided you seek them in marriage by giving them dowry from your property, desire virtuous character and not unlawful sexual intercourse. To enjoy marriage with them, give them their obligatory dowry. However, there is no harm in consensual compromise for the dowry…. (4:24)

> Believers, it is not lawful for you to inherit the widows of your deceased relative against their will. You should not treat them harshly in order to take back part of the dowry you gave them. …. (4:19)

> How could you take it [dowry] back while you both have sexual intercourse with each other and entered into a firm contract? (4:21)

Property Rights

A will is a legal declaration of a person's wishes for the disposal of his or her property or estate after death. God has specified shares for each family member, including daughters, wives, and widows.

In Islam, a person can write a will up to one-third of the estate. Two-thirds of the estate has to be distributed per the shares defined in the Quran. In Islam, a will is executed after payment of funeral expenses and outstanding debts. The one who makes a will is called a testator.

About a will, God has stated in the Quran:

> Those who die and leave widows behind should provide in their will a year's maintenance and residence for them. ...... (2:240)

God's orders for the distribution of your inheritance are:

- For children, a male's share will be twice of a female.
- If daughters only have two or more, their share is two-thirds. If one daughter only, her share is half.
- For parents, each has a sixth share if the deceased left children. If there are no children and the parents are the only heirs, the mother has a third. If the deceased left brothers or sisters, the mother has a sixth.
- The above distributions shall be after complying with the deceased's will and paying his debts. ..... (4:11)

And:

- Your share is half of what your wives leave if they leave no child. But if they leave a child, you get a fourth.
- Your wives' share is a fourth of what you leave, if you leave no child. But if you leave a child, they get an eighth.

- If the deceased has left neither parents nor children but has left a brother or a sister, each one gets a sixth. But if there are more than two, they share in a third.
- The above distributions shall be after complying with the deceased's will and paying his debts provided no loss is caused to anyone.

….. (4:12)

Sex

Per the Qur'an:

> You are prohibited from marrying married women except the war-captive slave women you own. …. All other women are lawful to you, provided …. you desire virtuous character and not unlawful sexual intercourse. …. (4:24)

> This day, the following have been made lawful for you:

> …. marriage to chaste women, both from believers and the People of the Book (Jews and Christians), when you give them their dowries, live in honor with them, do not commit fornication [sex between unmarried partners] and become their secret lovers. ….. (5:5)

> Those who find no means for marriage should stay away from sexual relations until God enriches them out of His grace. …. Do not force your slave girls into prostitution for you to earn money if they desire to keep themselves out of it. But if anyone would compel them, God will forgive the slave-girls and be merciful to them. (24:33)

> They ask you about menstruation. Say: It is an unclean state; keep away from women during it, and do not approach them for sex until they are clean. ….

> God will forgive and reward, both men and women, who ….

guard against their sexual desires, except from their wives or the slave-girls they possess, because they are lawful to them. (70:29-30)

Successful are the believers, who ... abstain from sexual relations, outside their marriages with free women or slave girls. For that, there is no blame on them. (23:1–6)

God created humanity through the marriage of Adam and Eve. In Islam, sexual relations are only permissible between legally married males and females. In the Quran, God has defined the conditions for permissible marriages. A dowry must be given to the wife and cannot be taken back in case of divorce. Sexual relations outside of marriage are considered sinful in Islam, and God punished Prophet Lot's nation for engaging in sexual relations with males.

Justice

According to the Qur'an:

> If any of your women commit illegal sexual intercourse, take the evidence of four witnesses from among you against them. If they testify to the allegation's truth, confine them to their houses until they die or God finds another way for them. (4:15)

> A hundred lashes should be given to an adulterer and an adulteress. No pity for them should make you disobey God, if you believe in God and the Last Day [of Judgment]. And let the believers witness their punishment. (24:2)

> Give 80 lashes to those who accuse honorable women without bringing out four witnesses, and never ever accept their testimony. They indeed are evildoers. Except those who repent and mend their ways. God is forgiving and merciful. If a man

accuses his wife of adultery but has no witness, he should testify four times in God's name that he is telling the truth. He should testify a fifth time for God's curse to be on him should he be lying. She will not be punished if she testifies four times in God's name that her husband was lying. Her fifth testimony should be for God's wrath to be upon her if she was lying. (24:4–9)

According to the above verses, extramarital sex is considered objectionable on social, religious, moral, and legal grounds. God has mandated the following:

- A hundred lashes should be given to an adulterer and an adulteress. No pity for them .... And let the believers witness their punishment.
- If any woman commits illegal sexual intercourse, take the evidence of four witnesses. If they testify to the allegation's truth, confine her to her house until she dies or God finds another way for her.

Per Dr. Iqbal:

- Men can't read a woman's mind.
- A husband and wife have differing body structures and roles.
- A woman is a lyre (stringed instrument) that can impart pathos (sadness) and warmth to a human heart.
- Her handful of clay is superior far to Pleiades (a bright cluster of stars) that so higher are for every man with knowledge vast like gem out of her cask (barrel) is cast.
- The likes of the Greek philosopher Plato were born by women.
- The women own great insight but are constrained and helpless, wise and sage, but cannot deal with their non-freedom in all spheres of life.
- It is an uphill task to judge what is more precious, lends much grace: Emancipation for fair sex or aught (nothing), or emerald-wrought superb neck-lace?

- A nation which can't protect its women soon begins to decline.
- If schools do not educate girls, then lore (knowledge) and crafts for love are indeed death.
- The spirit of man can display itself without obligation to another, But the spirit of woman cannot fully reveal itself without another's help. Teamwork is necessary.
- Her desire is the secret of her fever of sorrow: Her existence is full of fire with the wish to create.

Per Time Magazine:

In Time Magazine of April 29, 2024's list of The 100 Most Influential People Of The World includes 49 women out of 100:

In Time Magazine of May 13, 2024, list of The 100 Health Experts Of The World includes 40 women out of 100:

It is an impressive progress.

BIBLIOGRAPHY
Available @ Amazon.com

Akhtar A. Alvi, P.E.

- *The Qur'an, Islam's Holy Book, By Verse.*
- *The Qur'an, Islam's Holy Book, By Paragraph.*
- *Understanding God And His System.*
- *God's Guidance For Humans.*
- *God's Preaching Of His Religion.*
- *Understanding Human Nature And Eternal Life.*

Time Magazine of April 29 and May 13, 2024.

Wikipedia

Google.

APPENDIX

WOMAN
Dr. IQBAL's FEMISISM

http://iqbalurdu.blogspot.com/#zarbkaleem

1. Aurat - (عورت - مرد افرنگ) (Zarb-e-Kaleem-099) Mard-e-Afrang
2. Aik Sawal (ایک سوال) (Zarb-e-Kaleem-100)
3. Parda (پرده) (Zarb-e-Kaleem-101)
4. Khalwat (خلوت) (Zarb-e-Kaleem-102)
5. Aurat (عورت) (Zarb-e-Kaleem-103)
6. Azadi-e-Niswan (نسواں آزادی) (Zarb-e-Kaleem-104)
7. Aurat Ki (حفاظت کی عورت) (Zarb-e-Kaleem-105) Hifazat
8. Aurat Aur (تعلیم اور عورت) (Zarb-e-Kaleem-106) Taleem
9. Aurat (عورت) (Zarb-e-Kaleem-107)

Zarb-e-Kaleem-099) Aurat - Mard-e-Afrang

Aurat
Woman

**Mard-e-Farang
The Frankish Man
The British or European Man**

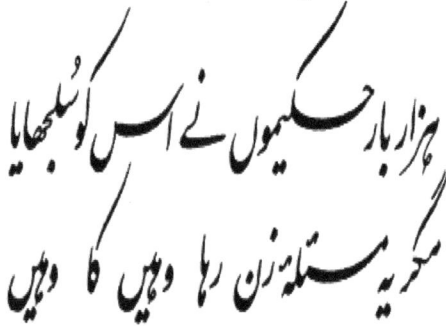

Hazar Bar Hakeemon Ne Iss Ko Suljhaya
Magar Ye Masla-e-Zan Raha Wahin Ka Wahin

To solve this riddle thinkers have much tried,
Their efforts all so far it has defied.

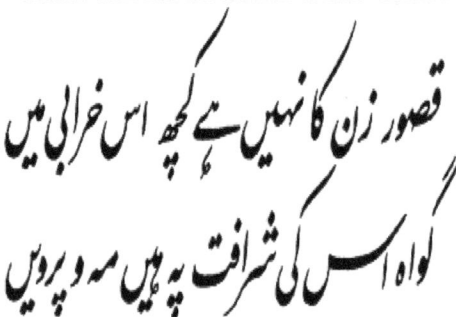

Qasoor Zan Ka Nahin Hai Kuch Iss Kharabi Mein
Gawah Iss Ki Sharafat Pe Hain Mah-o-Parveen

No doubt, to woman's faith and conduct clear,
The Pleiades* and moon do witness bear.

a group of stars that is one of the nearest to Earth

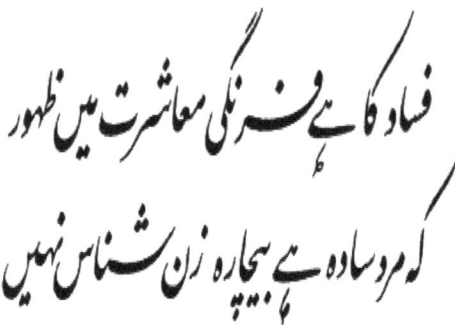

Fasad Ka Haifarangi Maasharat Mein Zahoor
Ke Mard Sada Hai Bechara Zan Shanas Nahin

This vice in the Frankish way of life we find,
Men fools and blind, can't read a woman's mind.

(Zarb-e-Kaleem-100) Aik Sawal

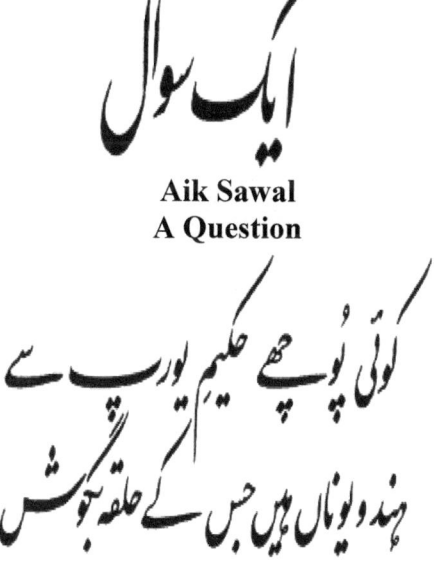

Aik Sawal
A Question

Koi Puche Hakeem-e-Yourap Se
Hind-o-Yunan Hain Jis Ke Halqa Bagosh

Ask the wise men of Europe, who have hung their ring in the nose of Greece and Hindustan:

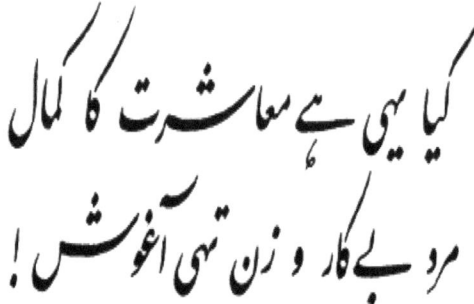

Kya Yehi Hai Maasharat Ka Kamal
Mard Bekaar-o-Zan Tehi Aagosh !

Is this their civilization's highest rung—
A childless woman and a jobless man?

(Zarb-e-Kaleem-101) Parda

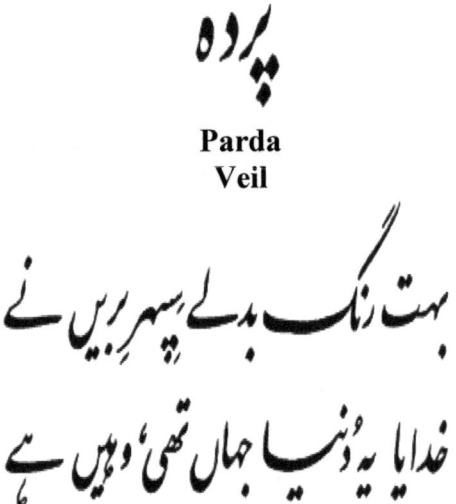

Parda
Veil

Bohat Rang Badle, Sipihr-e-Bareen Ne
Khudaya Ye Dunya Jahan Thi, Wahin Hai

(Sipihr = Aasman)

Great change the lofty spheres have met,
O God! the world has not budged as yet.

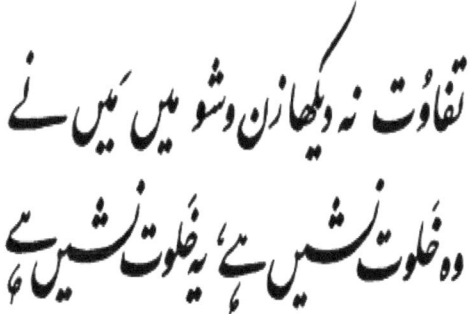

Tafawuf Na Dekha Zan-o-Sho Mein Main Ne
Woh Khalwat Nasheen Hai, Ye Khalwat Nasheen Hai

In man and wife is no contrast,
They like seclusion and hold it fast.

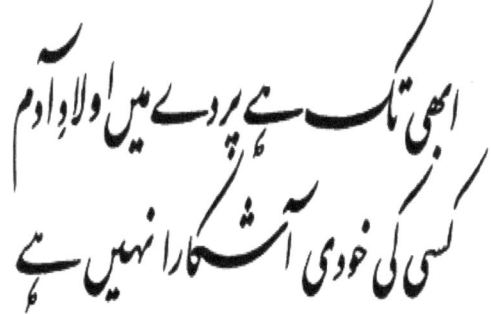

Abhi Tak Hai Parde Mein Aulad-e-Adam
Kisi Ki Khudi Ashakara Nahin Hai

The sons of Adam still wear the mask,
But self hasn't peeped out of the casque.

(Zarb-e-Kaleem-102) Khalwat

Khalwat
Solitude

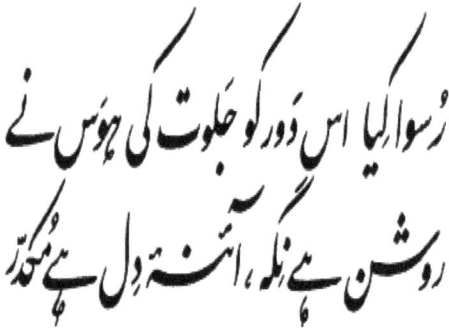

Ruswa Kiya Iss Dour Ko Jalwat Ki Hawas Ne
Roshan Hai Nigah, Aaeena-e-Dil Hai Mukaddar

(Mukaddar = Maila, Gadla)

Much greed for show and fame has put this age to shame:
The glance is bright and clear, Heart's mirror, but is clear.

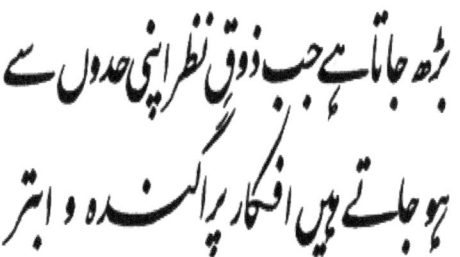

Barh Jata Hai Zauq-e-Nazar Apni Hadon Se
Ho Jate Hain Afkar Paraganda-o-Abtar

When zeal and zest for sight exceed their greatest height,
Thoughts soar to the highest point and soon are out of joint.

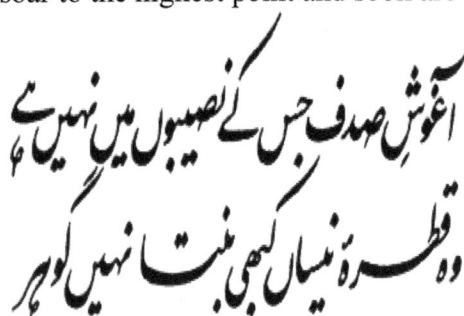

Aghosh-e-Sadaf Jis Ke Naseebon Mein Nahin Hai
Woh Qatra-e-Neesan Kabhi Banta Nahin Gohar

That vernal drop of rain the state of pearl can't gain
If destined not to dwell, In lap of mother shell.

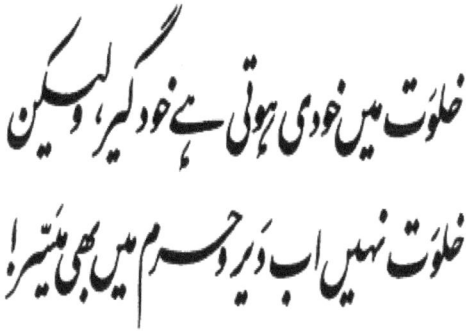

Khalwat Mein Khudi Hai Khudgeer, Walekin
Khalwat Nahin Ab Dair-o-Haram Mein Bhi Muyassar

Retreat is blessed state 'Bout self gives knowledge great:
Alas! this state divine, isn't found in fane or shrine.

(Zarb-e-Kaleem-103) Aurat

Aurat
Woman

Wujood-e-Zan Se Hai Tasveer-e-Kainat Mein Rang
Issi Ke Saaz Se Hai Zindagi Ka Souz-e-Darun

The picture that this world presents from woman gets its tints and scents:
She is the lyre that can impart pathos and warmth to human heart.

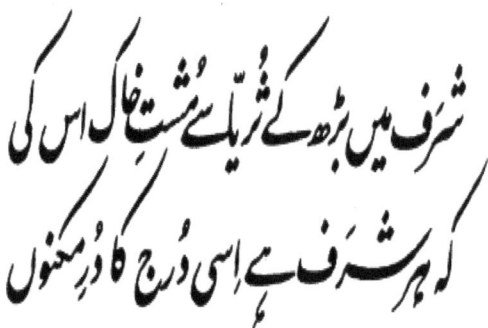

Sharaf Mein Barh Ke Sureya Se Musht-e-Khak Iss Ki
Ke Har Sharaf Hai Issi Durj Ka Dur-e-Makoon

Her handful clay is superior far to Pleiades that so higher are
For every man with knowledge vast, Like gem out of her cask is cast.

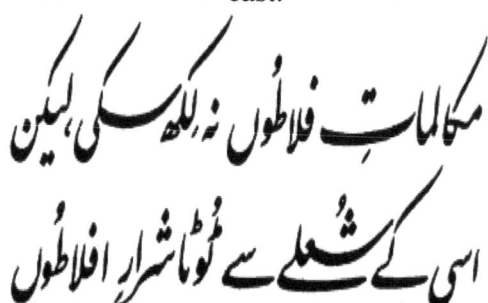

Makalat-e-Falatoon Na Likh Saki, Lekin
Issi Ke Shole Se Toota Sharaar-e-Aflatoon

Like Plato can not hold discourse, Nor can with thunderous voice declaim:
But Plato was a spark that broke from her fire that blazed like a flame.

(Zarb-e-Kaleem-104) Azadi-e-Niswan

Azadi-e-Niswan
Emancipation Of Women

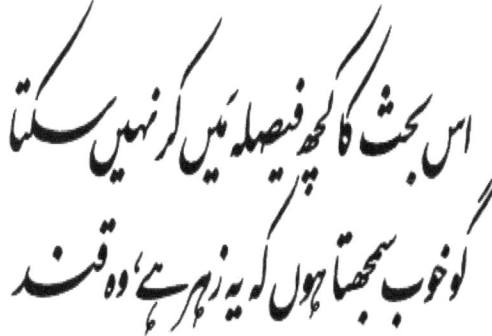

Iss Behas Ka Kuch Faisla Main Kar Nahin Sakta
Go Khoob Samajhta Hun Ke Ye Zaher Hai, Woh Qand

I know quite well that one despoils, While other is like candy sweet:
I can not give a verdict true which needs of Quest can fully meet.

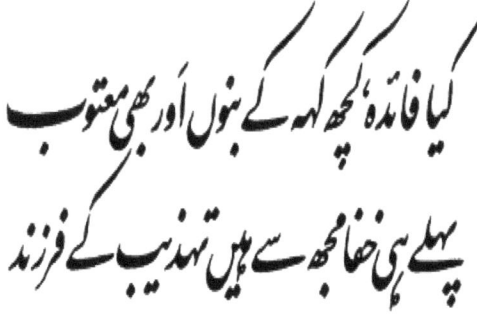

Kya Faida, Kuch Keh Ke Banon Aur Bhi Maatob
Pehle Hi Khafa Mujh Se Hain Tehzeeb Ke Farzand

I like to make no more remark and earn the wrath of present age:

Already the sons of modern cult 'Gainst me are full of ire and rage.

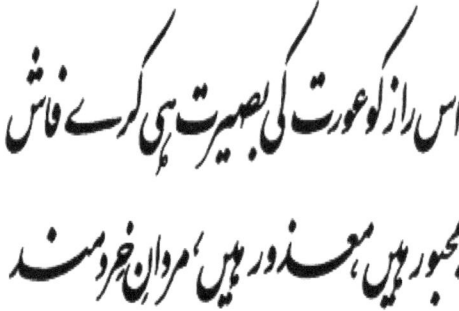

Iss Raaz Ko Aurat Ki Baseerat Hi Kare Faash
Majboor Hain, Maazoor Hain, Mardan-e-Khirdmand

The insight owned by woman can this subtle point with ease reveal:
Constrained and helpless, wise and sage, With knotty point they can not deal.

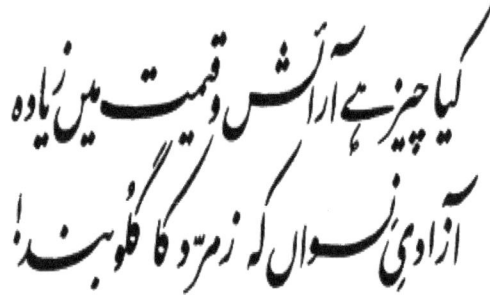

Kya Cheez Hai Araish-o-Qeemat Mein Zaida
Azadi-e-Niswan Ke Zumurd Ka Gluband !

It is an uphill task to judge what is more precious, lends much grace:
Emancipation for fair sex or aught, or emerald-wrought superb neck-lace?

(Zarb-e-Kaleem-105) Aurat Ki Hifazat

Aurat Ki Hifazat
Protection Of The Weaker Vessel

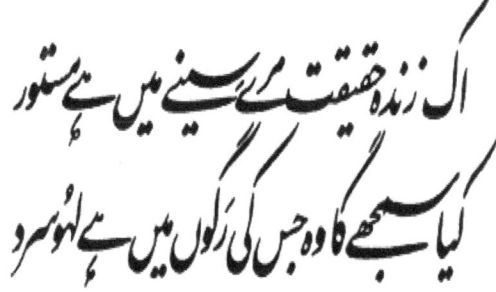

Ek Zinda Haqiqat Mere Seene Mein Hai Mastoor
Kya Samjhe Ga Woh Jis Ki Ragon Mein Hai Lahoo Sard

A fact alive is in my breast concealed,
He can behold whose blood is not congealed.

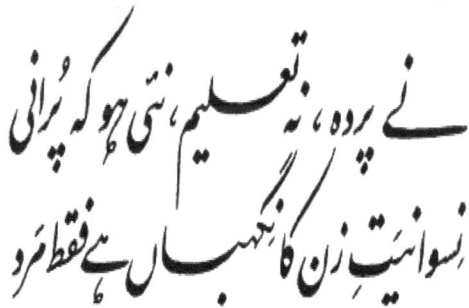

Ne Parda, Na Taleem, Nayi Ho Ke Purani
Niswaniyat-e-Zan Ka Nigheban Hai Faqt Mard

To wear a veil and learn new lore or old,
Can't guard fair sex except a person bold.

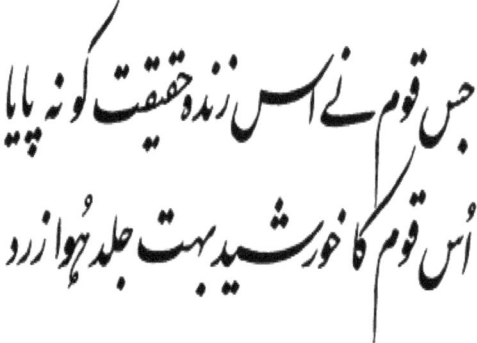

Jis Qoum Ne Iss Zinda Haqiqat Ko Na Paya
Uss Qoum Ka Khursheed Bohat Jald Huwa Zard

A nation which can't see this truth divine,
Pale grows its son and soon begins decline.

(Zarb-e-Kaleem-106) Aurat Aur Taleem

Aurat Aur Taleem
Education And Women

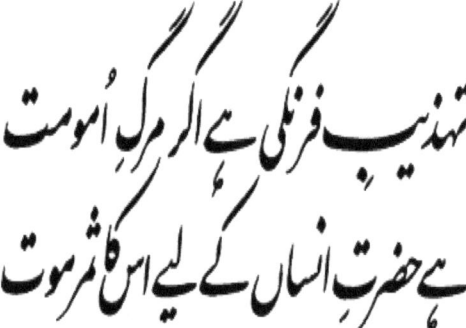

Tehzeeb-e-Farangi Hai Agar Marg-e-Umoomat
Hai Hazrat-e-Insan Ke Liye Iss Ka Samar Mout

If Frankish culture blights the motherly urge,
For human race it means a funeral dirge.

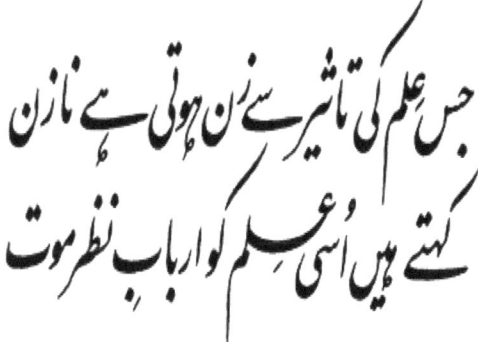

Jis Ilm Ki Taseer Se Zan Hoti Hai Na-Zan
Kehte Hain Ussi Ilm Ko Arbab-e-Nazar Mout

The lore that makes a woman lose her rank
Is naught but death in eyes of wise and frank.

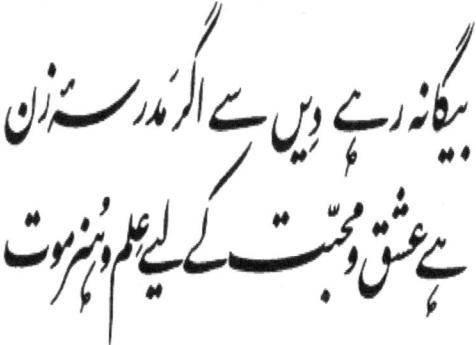

Begana Rahe Deen Se Agar Madrasa-e-Zan
Hai Ishq-o-Mohabbat Ke Liye Ilm-o-Hunar Mout

If schools for girls no lore impart on creed,
Then lore and crafts for Love are death indeed.
(Zarb-e-Kaleem-107) Aurat

Aurat
Woman

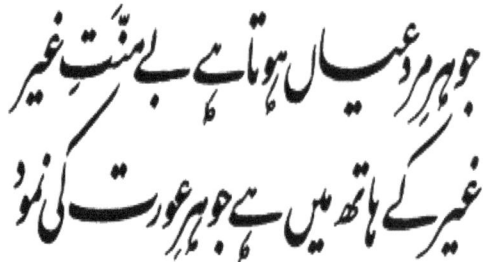

Johar-e-Mardayan Hota Hai Be Minnat-e-Ghair
Ghair Ke Hath Mein Hai Johar-e-Aurat Ki Namood

The spirit of man can display its self without obligation to another,
But the spirit of woman cannot fully reveal its self without another's help.

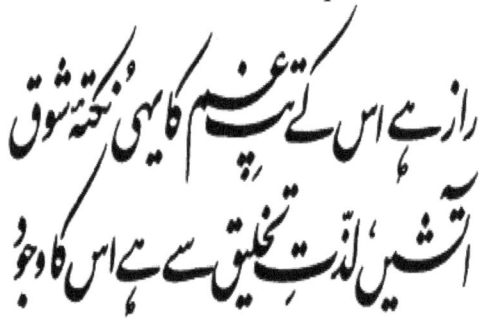

Raaz Iss Ke Tap-e-Gham Ka Yehi Nukta-e-Shauq
Atisheen, Lazzat-e-Takhleeq Se Hai Iss Ka Wujood

Her desire is the secret of her fever of sorrow:
Her existence is full of fire with the wish to create.

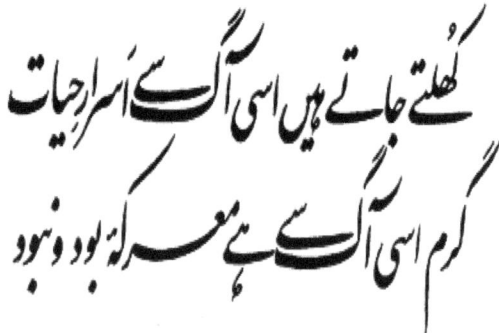

Khule Jate Hain Issi Aag Se Asrar-e-Hayat
Garam Issi Aag Se Hai Maarka-e-Bood-o-Nabood

Here is the fire which opens the secrets of life;
That is the heat which sustains the struggle between to be and not to be.

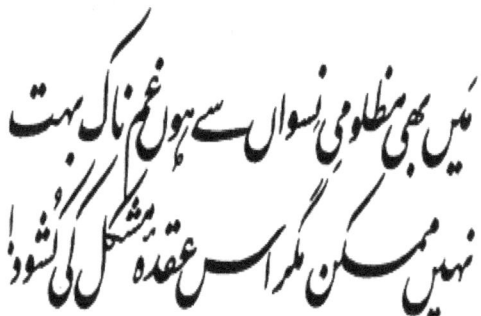

Mein Bhi Mazloomi-e-Niswan Se Hun Gham-Naak Bohat
Nahin Mumkin Magar Iss Uqda-e-Mushkil Ki Kushood!

I too feel sad about the oppression of women,
But this knotty problem cannot be resolved.

AUTHOR

Akhtar A. Alvi, P.E., is:
- An International Management Consultant.
- A retired civil and environmental engineer.
- A U.S. citizen of Pakistani origin.

He:
- Earned a Bachelor of Science and two Master of Science degrees in civil engineering from the University of Engineering & Technology, Lahore, Pakistan, and the Louisiana State University, Baton Rouge, Louisiana, USA.
- Taught civil engineering at the University of Engineering and Technology, Lahore, and Louisiana State University,
- Developed irrigation and hydropower projects for the Government of Nigeria and managed engineering and environmental projects for oil and gas companies in the United States and for the U.S. government.
- Mr. Alvi is the author of three books, which are available at Amazon.com.

www.ingramcontent.com/pod-product-compliance
Lightning Source LLC
LaVergne TN
LVHW070048070526
838201LV00036B/357